A KNOWABLE WORLD

SARAH WARDLE

A KNOWABLE WORLD

BLOODAXE BOOKS

Copyright © Sarah Wardle 2009

ISBN: 978 1 85224 819 2

First published 2009 by
Bloodaxe Books Ltd,
Highgreen,
Tarset,
Northumberland NE48 1RP.

www.bloodaxebooks.com
For further information about Bloodaxe titles
please visit our website or write to
the above address for a catalogue.

Bloodaxe Books Ltd acknowledges
the financial assistance of
Arts Council England, North East.

Cover design: Neil Astley & Pamela Robertson-Pearce.

Printed in Great Britain by
Bell & Bain Limited, Glasgow, Scotland.

*So many lives are not what they are meant
to be, and yet how else can days be learnt?*

ACKNOWLEDGEMENTS

Acknowledgements are due to the editors of the following publications, in which some of these poems first appeared: *Earls Court* ('Solitude', 'Christmas in October'), *The Interpreter's House* ('To my Grandmother'), *The London Magazine* ('Turquoise', 'Peace', 'Magnetic Resonance Imaging'), *Magma* ('Escape Route'), *Poetry Review* ('Found Audience', 'Healing', 'Snow from Ebury Ward'), *Read This Magazine* ('Psychiatrists Ask Questions'), *The Times Literary Supplement* ('Exchange', 'Life-Life Balance', 'After Ralph Vaughan Williams', 'Subject', 'Is', 'Leave') and *Women's Work*, ed. Eva Salzman & Amy Wack (Seren, 2008) ('Author! Author!').

'Hotel Gordon' has been brilliantly translated into Scots by Andrew Philip, and both poems were part of a diversity project for the 'The Language of Equality': *The Mayor's Annual Equalities Report 2006/07*. Thanks to organisers, Rogan Wolf and David Morris.

The first six poems of this book were broadcast on Channel S Television UK. Thanks to Hasan Hafizur Rahman, Munayem Mayenin and the London Poetry Festival.

'Sarah, wife of Abraham' is to be broadcast on BBC Radio 4 in February 2009. Thanks to Sara-Jane Hall.

Thank you to the British Council, Berlin, for my writing residency in September 2005.

CONTENTS

Magnetic Resonance Imaging

They asked me to lie down inside a tube,
which moved inside two walls of magnets, gave
me a panic button I didn't use,
although I longed to, trying to be brave.
Then for an hour loud sounds crashed and banged,
as I lay in this nuclear missile
of clinical white and my brain was scanned
for shading of schizophrenic detail.
There was none. I was cleared and taken off
anti-psychotics under supervision.
After a dozen years, I'd had enough.
What didn't show were bipolar symptoms.
I kept speaking poems I had written
to myself, trapped inside that white coffin.

At the Brandenburg Gate

On the city's pitch the Brandenburg Gate
stands like one goal, one aim, to be United,
let players pass, so none can relegate
another. And with no net, no score is counted.

Better to be whole and well than schizophrenic.
One needs to stick together to keep sane.
The lonely child who plays against a wall must kick
not just the football, but the frontier down.

Exchange

As I look at the postcard of a woman smiling,
I smile to recall my smile in the gallery,
when turning the corner, I smiled as on meeting,
on seeing the portrait of the woman smiling,

and for a moment became Frans Hals smiling,
eliciting a smile in return from the woman,
whom I now see in the card from the gallery,
as if she were alive again and smiling at me.

Peace

I write in praise of empty rooms,
a hall when a convention's gone,
a lecture theatre after term,
a deserted football ground,
a bath with water drained away,
a village church with no other presence,
the City's ghost town on Christmas Day,
poems declaimed to no audience,
the top of a hill at full moon,
a ward when others are asleep,
4 AM quiet, heard from a kitchen,
a Greek theatre's Atlantis deep,
streets with commuters gone to ground,
silence after a protest's sound.

Turquoise

Always a starting to the end,
reaching an island of pause,
never finding more than this
concentration on conscience,

the small difficulties of inner
ceasefire in a city of dreams,
the way days fold into each
other like museum postcards,

or an accordion of beer mats
inside a house of falling cards,
prophesying a future perfect
tense in a clause subordinate

to the main political concerns
of the day-to-day running of
the words behind the meaning
of things, always a sighting to

the last, like the geese arrow
of a fly-past, seen from shore,
always a beginning and never
a returning to the homes and

ones that have gone on before,
always this facing into a storm
on the flat edge of a knowable
world, which is yet unknown.

Found Audience

Faced with this train carriage, you want to recite to them,
lines of how the sunlight hits their office windowsills
just so, the concert of traffic below, discourses
of computer programmes and their accounts team,
the walk of the woman they desire, the man they conjure

by the vending machine. You want to speak
when you walk through London streets of the temples
that were here before the skyline spires, of the river
before it knew its name, of the land before people,
its primeval blood and mire. You want to listen

to daylight filtered through leaves, the stone of the city,
the dust of the place. You want to hear the voices
of those who worked here before you now, and left no trace.
You circle over familiar ground. Wherever you travel,
you reach a starting point, the beginning of ending.

You're an unreeled thread, spinning through weekdays
till the wheel's upright. Watch how these feet could belong
to another, as you walk the racecourse of the platform's length
and return to the starting gates, the ticket barrier to thought,
and pass through like a battery egg. The day's under

starter's orders and you're off in a world of dream-making
to the power of ten. You shoot down the escalator,
as if it's a playground slide, into the tunnel of ghost frowns.
The platform's three deep. The train's late. Silence
expands to fill the lack of space. You badly need

to read *Four Quartets* or the *Sonnets to Orpheus*
in each person's face. But here, before the London terminus,
you want to say only that ringed dates draw nearer,
like six o'clock departure, or these trees now
speeding into lost distance, becoming the green future

you'll drive at this evening under purple skies, preparing
for another sleep, the pentameter of the rail ever broken in half
by the caesura of a change of track, the way the echo answers
back, as heads loll and they are lulled by rhythmic comfort,
catching up on missed life. You want to tell them that.

Don't Try This *Not* At Home

First, arriving very early to work,
opening your office Fire Exit,
wandering distractedly around the campus,
arguing with Security in the car park,
because it leads to police and an ambulance.

Second, approaching a group of policemen
to ask why a WPC is haranguing
a member of the public in the street,
because they will ask you very nicely
to step into the back of their van,
drive you to detention and then a clinic.

Third, heading in the wrong direction
in rush hour on the Piccadilly Line,
then chipping into some coppers' conversation,
because, though you'll be let off without a caution,
the police will give you a lift to work,
where your line-manager will be waiting,
having cancelled your lecture and your class.

Fourth, protesting against a march
a policeman has told you is about terrorism,
lifting up the white tape and shouting
back at an oncoming crowd about victims,
because an officer, drafted in from Romford,
will arrest you and ask you to sit in his van
and you'll have to direct his out-of-town clan
to your local station, before a clinic and detention.

Fifth, arguing with a tube train driver
after a football match on New Year's Eve
to ask why the train isn't moving,
when you'd forgotten all about red lights,
after two years not driving, using the Underground,
because he'll call the station guards,
and though the British Transport Police
will let you go, you might not have been able to share
your centenarian grandmother's last New Year.

And sixth, asking a man to switch off his phone,
arguing with a ticket man and guard on a train,
proving that your ticket is valid
and that you have a right to travel,
that you'll not disembark unless UK Law says you have to,
because that way you'll have set the Sussex Police
upon yourself, and when you accuse them of malpractice,
they'll arrest you and drive you miles to a cell,
where you'll be interviewed by a panel
and the next morning carted off for a year in hospital.

Harrowing

After two injections by night I fled the clinic,
escaping through a narrow bathroom window,
shoeless, without change, with clothes ripped,
getting as far as the gated tube at South Harrow
before going back to face the music.

Bloomburg Street

Bloomburg Street was the sign I glimpsed
from a ward window, wondering where I was.
Its name rang with hope, not merely ice,
but the breaking through of the year's rites.

Sarah, wife of Abraham

(after Lorna Goodison)

I am becoming my grandmothers,
white-haired with the knowledge of time,
making a beginning of ending
in the impossible country of life,
eating onions and ginger to ward off death,

delving into a sewing bag of moments
for threads of memory, beads loose as teeth,
old buttons from the 1930s, a bodice
she'll never step into twice, twin
magnifying glasses, one wireless, one radio,

tuned to Radio 4 and the World Service,
their own mothers, framed in sepia and white,
Victorian pillars bearing up the generations
of daughters now ninety and a century,
my mother, father, bachelor uncle, spinster aunt,

but no brother, sister, or first cousin,
with whom to pass through,
since I am the one space beneath the arch,
realising that the gates are now closing,
that I may never be an elder, a matriarch.

New Year's Eve, 2005

I am heading back from a football match,
when I argue with a tube train driver,
but a Glaswegian British Transport Officer
lets me go to my father's 100 year-old mother,
advising me to seek some care.
I say, 'They didn't have counselling in the war.'

For Great Uncle Hugh

(4 January 2006)

I can't forgive myself for not paying you a visit
as you lay dying in a nursing home in Dorset,
and after your decline and death was kept a secret,
on a train back to London I wept and wept,
before arguing with police and resisting arrest.

Unnatural Justice

They arrest you, though you called for the Law,
since you thought they'd be your support,
after arguing with a train guard,
showing him your ticket was valid,

but they handcuff you and drive you miles
to a town you'll never see in light
and stick you in a cell, so you shout
to them to back off, but they don't

and six of them push you down on a mat
and twist your arms behind your back,
and that, Ladies and Gentlemen, is justice,
as delivered by the Police so-called Service.

Wild Card

You shout to a pack of men to go away,
even move a wardrobe as a barricade,

but bureaucratic duty to obey the book
dictates that empathy and insight get overlooked

and it's more than some people's jobs are worth
to open a locked door, or grant a wide berth.

Healing

In art therapy I do not draw a picture,
but write my name with my left hand,
Greek letters backwards, as in a mirror,
and in English, 'I can! I can! I can! I can!'.

Mother's Flowers

Daffodils in this drab room
trumpet not only spring,
but an end to these weeks of gloom,
when I'll again be walking

clear of this section order.
These flowers represent the sun,
a time when Ceres' daughter
rejoins family, life and freedom.

S 3

I'm a tree with a ball and chain,
rooted to the lino in this prison,
sea-blue, like the flood that will digest
us all, if the fire doesn't catch us first.
When the alarm bell rang, not a soul
knew if it were a practice, or for real.
'Responsible' by any other name
is the RMO and his decision
to detain us, deploying his power game,
when each of us is his own physician
and can cure himself. Yet try telling that
to psychiatrists, the most obstinate
profession, making a person doubt his mind,
though all comes calm, given space and time.

Life-Life Balance

Great stories begin and fade to close,
as if the silence of the summer knows
and deep in night's 4.48 psychosis,
when suicides drop from Blackfriars Bridge,
I bear with a city, not wholly asleep,
whilst someone drives sheep through a tower gate.

Flash

He was the gelding I felt sorry for,
though highest in the horses' pecking order,
until that day he took me out at a gallop
across an open field of stubble crop.

I felt that pulse rate of panic again,
when cornered by nine West Midlands policemen,
after doctors had called me back to hospital,
doubting my ability to stay in life's saddle.

Conversion

I count my love for him in old age coins.
He is my florin, my crown, my pound, my guinea.
Without him near, I am but half a crown.
Apart, I am two farthings, or a halfpenny.

At one, we are each a threepence piece,
conjoining together to make up a sixpence,
yet however I account for him, his love
lies both in what he says and what he does.

Eurydice

You are Orpheus, descending to the hell
of visiting time in this mental hospital,
reassuring me with the rhythm you bring
from the world of felt sunshine, rain and wind,

calming my tone and pressure of speech
with your pitch of patience, tenor of touch.
As you look over your shoulder to say goodbye,
I stay, as I have from January to July.

Leave

It's been a long time since I've been home.
Even now I'm just on leave, visiting.
I gather the last dried traces of spring,
primroses, daffodils, a branch's blossom,
and carry them down in a bag to the bin,
as if they were my grandmother's confetti remains,
remembering how I looked up at the sun
on the morning after the night she passed on,
and on the ward, unaware she was dying,
shouting, 'I hereby annul my baptism.'

Is

The problem of tenses when someone has died,
even on the anniversary of their death,
is like the correct translation of John,
which is 'kept on weeping', not merely 'wept'.

Author! Author!

Readers, know that writing is a private pleasure.
Each of you may interpret these words together,
yet the key to these usages, here, remains with me,
for it is your very absence that lets this poem be,
and though individually these words are public,
only the weaver understands their interrelationship,
so that these lines serve as blinds, or prison bars,
to keep an audience distant, guessing from afar,
while I remain inside my poem, mind and state,
for understand this print is not blood spilt on a page,
but, what is more uncanny, space beneath the stone,
a translation, chiselled in sand, hollowed on a tomb,
wherein lie the silent bones of this white sheet,
taking with them their true, unverified secret.

Handwriting

Left alone in the group room one evening,
I found tubes of paint in yellow and pink
and marked twenty handprints on the ceiling,
like cave art, to make the doctors think.

Escape Route

For how long she hated him because he caused
her grandmother's death through negligence
to release her in time to make a difference,
and so she argued at him and the law,
which bound her here and took away her freedom,
as if she were a trapped lioness, or pigeon,
flying at a cage, or window frame.
Another patient diagnosed Stockholm syndrome
and she had certainly begun to love him,
harming her relationship with her lover,
dreaming of a man, who must be a father,
because, despite her hate, she knew him kind,
and though she saw no ring on either hand,
the truth was in the way he showed command.

After Having Been AWOL

Perhaps it was the way it never would
progress to anything other else than pain,
which explained the way she'd think of him again,
locked up nightly with his absence from the ward.
Perhaps it was the way for months they'd argued,
which lent the drama a hint of bittersweet,
and though she knew she'd never be complete
with him, each lonely night he seemed her target.
Perhaps it was his smile and body when, near,
she'd glimpse him for ten minutes on a Thursday,
or was it something in the goodwilled way
that first morning he had calmed her from her fear,
or when the fire practice alarm bells rang,
he had seemed to sense her panic and understand.

Trust Core Values

The consultant psychiatrist is on the ward.
In his proximity, all is hope with the world.
Through a door's porthole I catch a glimpse
of him discussing patients with nursing staff,
seated like a pupil, yet chairing his meeting,
his face, like a professor's, flushed with talking,
managing to speak back with a wordless glance,
although nothing is there but coincidence,
yet the fear, panic and hatred are gone,
even in a world rocked by wrong,
and everything left is right and trust,
even when love is not returned,
since his Scottish blue eyes are a beacon,
which simultaneously dispel and beckon.

The Semantics of Psychiatry

The nurse informs me the love I feel
is excess dopamine, nothing real,
and though I have been long acquainted
with crushes which are unrequited,
sensations override her science,
whilst daydreams keep me in a trance,
until I am at a loss to fathom
what is true and what is bunkum,
and though I promise to comply
with medication to make me docile,
conscience says my infatuation
is a case of meta-medication,
hyper-physical, beyond illness,
reproduction the diagnosis.

To My Grandmother

Although my grandmother has failing sight,
she teaches me to see clearly and take
medication the doctor says is right,
so I shall never make the same mistake
and leave myself open to mania,
which overcomes me when I stop the pills,
so that to my Oedipus, or King Lear,
she plays Tiresias, or the wise Fool,
for she, herself, has had a pacemaker,
and transfusion after a haemorrhage,
been saved by an operating theatre,
and hands me down the knowledge of her age,
so that I am better equipped to live
and pass on life to help her genes survive.

Subject

The more you look, the more each Van Gogh sunflower
betrays his escalation into mania.
The fullness of the spheres, which spin with relish,
are at odds with scarecrows, which no longer flourish.
The sorrow of the life cycle is what leaves
the viewer contemplating bloom to seeds,
while the golds as bright as fields of summer corn
lie beside his name in black on the vase ash-urn.
He hasn't depicted roses, bud to wilt,
but something far more stark to mark the melt
of human flesh from youth to not just age,
but death and rebirth through each centrifuge.
Each sunflower becomes a dandelion,
whose clock counts down his life and health of mind.

Psychiatrists Ask Questions

Just as Hume questioned if the sun won't rise,
may I ask you, though you cannot reply
due to your strict professionalism,
what if there'd been light this side of heaven
and I had been given another life?
Might I have borne you bairns and been your wife,

ironed your shirts for ward rounds, cooked your supper,
played mother alongside God the Father
to a family of seven, or eight?
If stars were other, might you impregnate
me, whilst I lie back and think of Scotland?
For I'd campaign and urge you on to stand

to represent in an English body
looks I've learnt by heart, and voice by proxy,
letting north Britannia rule my gaze,
your cold-front blue eyes and your shock of grey,
willing you invade my southern climate
with kilt. Were you not my psychiatrist,

but a Samaritan I'd met one day,
might a younger me have led you astray,
finding in your smile and body, when near,
a way to overcome my stupid fear,
conjoining, through a different transference,
to produce and outlast this world of chance?

If you were placed above and over me,
though not in a position of authority,
then without demanding my compliance,
you'd have my freely-given consensus,
so that I'd agree your every whim,
for in the battle of minds you know you win.

Might we have established a causal link
between prior action and consequence,
so you might have been my next of kin,
married by priests, who were our offspring?
Might you have made of me a convert
from the enlightenment to the kirk?

If you were to sense half the love I do
and have existed centuries ago,
might you have been Robbie Burns and left me
amongst harvest skies and rigs of barley?
Might you have met me coming through the rye,
be it as unlikely as that the sun could die?

Hope's Café

Meeting my psychiatrist on a street corner,
I smile madly and am lost for words.
Seeing this man who had been my gaoler,
I wish him well and that he, 'Take care!'
Transference is the name one calls it
for someone to whom one becomes bonded
through their kindness and their wit,
for in normal life you would feel befriended.
And like a Kylie pop song chord,
I can't get that psychiatrist out of my head.
When home, I act as if after a ward round
and go straight away to lie down on my bed,
behaving like a star-struck teen,
although I'm all of thirty-seven.

Outpatient

'Like love, misery is blind,'
the doctor says poetically,
back from sun and sand,
profiting from psychiatry
and misfortunes of the mad.

I wonder if he's ever been sad,
if successful men know sorrow,
if the fortunate ever truly love,
when there's nothing they feel they need to prove,
when they've never feared tomorrow.

Hospital Radio

Twice now I've been back in hospitals,
these times as a visitor, sure I can get out.

The blue and white NHS signs feel like home,
or motorway exits. Turn right at Cardiology

for your next junction. The closest service station
is miles away. The traffic is stalled

across all three lanes. Switch on the radio.
Keep going. By now you know how.

A Dialogue Between the Body and the Soul

I have made you what you are.
Without my cells, you'd not exist.
My synapses, lungs and heart
sustain you out of nothingness.

Without me, you'd have no guide.
You'd be left without a conscience.
I'm the one who can decide
to abandon you to madness.

Leave me and you'd have no voice.
My ears do, or do not, listen
to you when you offer choice.
You are trapped inside my prison.

No. I'm free and give you freedom
to respond to life's dilemmas.
Without me, you'd have no reason.
I'm the one who lives forever.

Undated, *circa* 1910-1914

On a gallery wall a woman photographer
has handed to us a London summer,
red geraniums, entitled *Brighter*.
Was it taken before the First World War?
It is ten to three. I think of 'Granchester',
wonder at red, like fields of Flanders,
startled by how the camera captures
a London hotter than it's been this year.
I can almost smell their earthy leaves,
fanned out around the reaching stems.
There is no shadow, cast by trees.
The woman's gaze and camera lens
want us to know, not just believe,
a garden blossomed and would again.

After Ralph Vaughan Williams

The Lark Ascending is my parents' lives,
running the currents of the skies,
buffeted by each downward blow,
riding the eddies of air below,

as if each upturn and turbulence
is caused by me and is my fault,
but the music's pity is that the flight
ends in their spirit rising out of sight.

Christmas in October

This October I have bought a Christmas tree,
longing to be back on the ward,
and where my flat once felt lonely,
a presence fills it, like a Druid god.
For a year I was sectioned and wanted freedom,
so now it comes as a surprise
that I am recreating the asylum
as it was last year at Christmastime.
But on the ward I never once felt solitude,
though anger, boredom and frustration ran
through my veins. Now this verisimilitude
of nurses' and patients' company is my friend.
I sit and watch its pin-lights like a fire,
sensing it warm me, when my soul had tired.

At Epiphany

I am done with thinking about death,
afraid to go to bed, lest a grandmother die.
I lost one, as if I had lost a breast.
There's no spirit, only the signified.
I stare at the certainty of a pine table.
o mensa. I no longer believe in Forms,
jealous of the toughness of which wood is capable,
surefooted solidity outstripping lifetimes.

But on the table a blue jug of tulips
reminds me there's still life. Bottled wine
speaks of leafy vineyards, bunches, pips
to seed new summers, just as humankind
in the shape of my lover stirs from his bedroom sleep,
sits at the now functional table with food and drink.

Ten Questions My Psychiatrist Never Asks

How often do you daydream about me?
Does the feeling last for hours? Weeks?

Do my clothes remind you of your father?
Are you aware I'm not old enough to be your father?

Would you like me to tell you about my life?
You do know I divorced my wife?

How many times do you look at my eyes? Lips? Hair?
Shall we take some Viagra together?

Did you know this room is booked for twenty minutes?
Why don't you move into a closer seat?

Recipe for Disability

Take the symptoms of mania.
Add a crush on a consultant. Stir

well. Reduce the dose of valium.
Spice with nurses visiting one's home,

then social workers, a crisis team.
Marinate in an assessment for a section.

Freeze for weeks on a mental ward
past the use-by date. Then discard.

PRN

Pro re nata medication,
given by nurses on a whim,
feels like sexual violation.
First you try to blockade your room,

then are pushed prone on a mattress,
or down on lino you're unzipped.
Despite your bellows of distress,
the needle rapes you with its prick.

S 136

If the police find someone 'mentally disordered',
they can take them to a so-called 'place of safety',
where you can be toxically medicated
and detained for months without judge, or jury.

Today a man pissed in the dining-room.
A patient downstairs is dealing crack.
A workman told me someone on observation
hanged herself from a window latch.

NHS

The first night I was admitted to The Gordon
I'd spent the day in St Ann's, Tottenham,
and when I was out of the ambulance,
I ran off to a locked gate, barking, 'Back!',

then sprinted away to the square's railings,
called the police on 999,
shouting, 'Each of you individually back off!',
but was marched into the hospital entrance,

where I stood by the locked doors, shouting, 'Open!',
while surrounded by eight, or nine, tall men,
was eventually dragged to a lift and a bed
and told to swallow, still surrounded,

while a patient ran up to try to help me,
was tackled to the floor. 'He could be my baby,'
I said, feigning madness, wandering out of my room
to hold his hand, as he lay in the scrum.

Hotel Gordon

An Irishman with holes in his boots,
fresh from the soup kitchen and Victoria station,
a South African, sleeping in night buses,

visitors, not even speaking the language
of the country, let alone the sense of sanity,
women with histories of sad adoptions,

a man from Eton, addicted to drink and crack,
a black man, knifed, and abused as a child,
yet gentle as the father he became at sixteen,

an Italian who lost her mother aged four:
all these I mean, people lost in the in between
of life, as some make good and others fall back.

From Room 3

Saturday is quiet. Patients on leave
and doctors at home make the place feel spare,
whilst I try to preserve my sanity
by sending poems to myself on paper.

Rows of terraced houses seem contented,
as I look out, deprived of liberty.
An aeroplane is roaring overhead.
Wind shakes the topmost branches of the trees.

Breaktime treble no longer fills a court.
A black crow caws five times for company.
A flock of pigeons startles into flight.
Last term's football pitch lies worn and empty.

The pavilion presides over the field.
A council tower block pierces the air.
Groundsmen roll the grass to make it yield.
Horses' ringing hooves circle the square.

British Summer Time begins tomorrow.
I've only three more days left on the ward.
Branches' shoots burst forth from winter's sorrow.
I cannot see the sky for gathering cloud.

Solitude

It is in words that I have found patience,
locked on a ward with language's silence.
Left by a radiator with one's thoughts,
sunrise and car tail lights become one's prompts.

It is the pauses of the day which bring
punctuation to consciousness' meaning.
Light plays on the grass and for an instance
ideas are grasped and become a sentence.

Treetops fan out, each twig like a dendrite,
while impulsive nerves impel me to write.
A pair of mating crows are back again,
speaking in the warning caws of madmen.

Darkness has again fallen in the square
on those in hospital forgotten here.
For others daffodils bloom and the sun
today warmed the skin of ones with freedom.

It is in dialogue with one's own mind
lonely conversations begin to find
a way from illness and fragility
to the sanity of stability.

Mind Games

The ward is empty where your smile's been,
the group room, multi-disciplinary team
room, the nursing station, kitchen, corridor,
all backdrops where you've breathed and walked before
so many times, your clinic in a nearby street,
in which you meet with every outpatient,
the main road where I once glimpsed you walk
to your bus stop, glad as a boy to have finished work.
Now there are only spaces I've seen you fill,
as if your soul-doctor's spirit haunts this hospital,
your ghost still running up a flight of stairs,
while your body is miles away and unaware,
or your stance, stressed, speaking on the phone,
though the conversation's over and you're long gone.

Snow from Ebury Ward

Each snowflake is a minute of detainment,
filling the air with falling measures of time,
not settling, but hitting the ground to melt,
like wasted hours, sectioned for losing one's mind.
Sometimes the wind eddies the snowflakes upwards
and they take longer to sink, as moments stall,
like the sensation that time is going backwards,
that we're forgotten and no hope's left at all.
But somewhere in me there is still delight
to see each snowflake, as in a Midlands winter.
And though down south it doesn't stick, the sight
of snow in March gives us a white Easter.
By lunchtime there's no trace, but half a day
has been ticked off the time I'll spend away.

For Michelle Farrell

The day after you drank vodka and died
the sky was like the colour of your eyes.
All morning I felt glad to be alive,
although locked up interminably inside.
The ward is still filled by your Irish spirit,
like the time you called the doctor a 'Fuckwit'.
If only when he'd offered you a bed,
you'd gone back to your hotel room instead.
You were not depressive, manic, schizophrenic,
but fighting delusions of an alcoholic.
This hospital was not the place for you.
They kept calling. There was nothing they could do.
Paramedics, police, forensics came.
You're gone. I sense you living all the same.

For Phil

You had a drunken fall and that was when
I realised I was doing you no good
these two months with your vodka and white wine,
because you don't like doing what you should.
We sat in A and E three days running.
They put you on a drip of vitamins.
Operations then restored your hearing.
I emptied my spare room, packed up your things.
I want to say I saw your father cry,
as he said that you would need to hit rock bottom
before you'd find the strength again to try
to quit and start to rebuild your good fortune.
He mentioned your sister, of whom I'd never heard,
despite the fact I've known you twenty years.

On Ben Nevis

I am walking in my psychiatrist's country.
I've left the group, as it makes for the summit,
content to go slow with my own company.
I set my goals too high and yet
how would I have reached this halfway plateau
and waterfall, if I hadn't aimed
at higher things? The ascent from below
so far has balanced pleasure and pain.
Why climb a mountain? We fill in time
as we can. Wind blows through the cotton grass.
We create adventure for body and mind,
like this scribbling here by a rocky path,
mindful of danger in descent to come,
as helicopter and ambulance rescue someone.